STAND OUT

THE TRUE STORY OF HOCKEY HERO AJAY BAINES

A team effort by Ajay Baines and Sean Campbell

Illustrated by Lana Lee

To God, my family, and my hockey family. - Ajay

For My Mom. For Everything - Sean

More info at www.seancampbellauthor.com

STAND OUT

1. A person of exceptional ability

2. Easily noticeable

From his first hockey book
To a cold icy pond,
Ajay and this game
Formed a very strong bond.

How could anyone not
Love this beautiful game?
It is all about the crest
And not your last name.

Hockey gave him confidence
A better body, mind, and soul.
Great friendships and mentors
And even sometimes a goal.

It also gave him stitches
A few holes in his smile.
All a small price to pay
It was worth it by a mile.

Ajay played game after game
With focus, fire, and pride.
Felt the power and bond of
Great teammates at his side.

There was even great rivals
Who would grind and pound.
In the end, show respect
With handshakes all around.

In the best shape of his life,
He could play hard for hours.
But then something felt off:
He had fading superpowers.

So off to the doctor.
Surely, with nothing to fear?
But then came the grim news
He did not want to hear.

Diabetes was a word
He didn't know much about,
But somehow he knew
Another way to stand out.

Diabetes: a disease that affects how the body uses glucose, a sugar that is the body's main source of fuel.

At this limitless age
Kids can almost have it all,
But so often all they
Want is a puck or a ball.

Diabetes was tough.
But no match for Ajay.
He kept moving forward,
Making progress each day.

He made some mistakes, not
Always sure what to do.
But had help from docs, family,
And some awesome trainers too.

Not easy for sure, but
He had so many gifts.
With new tech he could check
His blood between shifts.

No matter what roadblocks
Seemed to get in his way,
Ajay just worked harder
Making play after play.

He inspired the best.
To be all they could be,
So on team after team
He was given the "C".

Beside All-Star teammates
He boldly played his role.
In his biggest moment
He scored his biggest goal!

A standout all his life
In many unique ways.
He grabbed hold of the cup...

And gave it a raise.

In 2007, Ajay Baines scored the game winning goal to help the Hamilton Bulldogs win the Calder Cup. His perseverance, his successes and failures, and all of his hard work culminated in this incredible moment. It was a major highlight from an illustrious career playing with some of hockey's best.

" As a first year pro hockey player, I was lucky to have a leader like Ajay on my team. He always had my back and looked out for us younger guys all the time."

- Duncan Keith

3 Time Stanley Cup Winner
2 Time Olympic Gold Medallist
2 Time Norris Trophy Winner
Conn Smythe Trophy Winner
No. Big. Deal.

After a long playing career, life-long friendships, and the fire of competition, Ajay now lives with his amazing family in Kamloops, BC. He has transitioned into refereeing... his two kids for misconduct and roughing penalties. They are the whole world.

Manufactured by Amazon.ca
Bolton, ON

34024970R00019